ALTO SAX

IRVING BERLIN'S

God Bless America
& Other Patriotic Favorites

T0059221

Contents

ABOUT "GOD BLESS AMERICA"

"GOD BLESS AMERICA" by Irving Berlin was first published in 1938. Almost as soon as the song began generating revenue, Mr. Berlin established The God Bless America Fund to benefit American youth.

Over $6,000,000 has been distributed to date, primarily to two youth organizations with which Mr. and Mrs. Berlin were personally involved: the Girl Scout Council of Greater New York, and the Greater New York Councils of the Boy Scouts of America. These councils do not discriminate on any basis and are committed to serving all segments of New York City's diverse youth population.

The trustees of The God Bless America Fund are working with the two councils to ensure that funding is allocated for New York City children affected by the tragic events of September 11, 2001.

ISBN 0-634-04023-5

HAL•LEONARD®
CORPORATION

7777 W. BLUEMOUND RD. P.O. BOX 13819 MILWAUKEE, WI 53213

Visit Hal Leonard Online at
www.halleonard.com

AMERICA, THE BEAUTIFUL

ALTO SAX

Words by KATHERINE LEE BATES
Music by SAMUEL A. WARD

ANCHORS AWEIGH

ALTO SAX

Words by ALFRED HART MILES and ROYAL LOVELL
Music by CHARLES A. ZIMMERMAN

THE BATTLE CRY OF FREEDOM

ALTO SAX

Words and Music by
GEORGE FREDERICK ROOT

BATTLE HYMN OF THE REPUBLIC

ALTO SAX

Words by JULIA WARD HOWE
Music by WILLIAM STEFFE

THE CASSIONS GO ROLLING ALONG

ALTO SAX

Words and Music by
EDMUND L. GRUBER

COLUMBIA, THE GEM OF THE OCEAN
(The Red, White And Blue)

ALTO SAX

By DAVID T. SHAW

ETERNAL FATHER, STRONG TO SAVE

ALTO SAX

Words by WILLIAM WHITING
Music by JOHN BACCHUS DYKES

GOD BLESS AMERICA

ALTO SAX

Words and Music by
IRVING BERLIN

HAIL TO THE CHIEF

ALTO SAX

By JAMES SANDERSON

LIBERTY BELL MARCH

ALTO SAX

By JOHN PHILIP SOUSA

MARINE'S HYMN

ALTO SAX

Words by HENRY C. DAVIS
Melody based on a theme by
JACQUES OFFENBACH

MY COUNTRY, 'TIS OF THEE
(America)

ALTO SAX

Words by SAMUEL FRANCIS SMITH
Music from THESAURUS MUSICUS

NATIONAL EMBLEM

ALTO SAX

By E.E. BAGLEY

OVER THERE

ALTO SAX

Words and Music by
GEORGE M. COHAN

Medium March Tempo (♩ = 100)

SEMPER FIDELIS

ALTO SAX

By JOHN PHILIP SOUSA

SEMPER PARATUS

ALTO SAX

Words and Music by
CAPT. FRANCIS SALTUS VAN BOSKERCK, USCG

THE STAR SPANGLED BANNER

ALTO SAX

Words by FRANCIS SCOTT KEY
Music by JOHN STAFFFORD SMITH

STARS AND STRIPES FOREVER

ALTO SAX

By JOHN PHILIP SOUSA

THIS IS A GREAT COUNTRY

ALTO SAX

Words and Music by
IRVING BERLIN

THIS IS MY COUNTRY

ALTO SAX

Words by DON RAYE
Music by AL JACOBS

THIS IS THE ARMY, MR. JONES

ALTO SAX

Words and Music by
IRVING BERLIN

THIS LAND IS YOUR LAND

ALTO SAX

Words and Music by
WOODY GUTHRIE

THE THUNDERER

ALTO SAX

By JOHN PHILIP SOUSA

THE U.S. AIR FORCE

ALTO SAX

Words and Music by
ROBERT CRAWFORD

WASHINGTON POST MARCH

ALTO SAX

By JOHN PHILIP SOUSA

YANKEE DOODLE

ALTO SAX

TRADITIONAL

YANKEE DOODLE BOY

ALTO SAX

Words and Music by
GOERGE M. COHAN

YOU'RE A GRAND OLD FLAG

ALTO SAX

Words and Music by
GEORGE M. COHAN